WORLD OF ROBOTS

WILD ROBOTS

Book 2.

To Curtis, enjoy the books!

Written by
JOE CRAIG

Illustrated by
Dylan Gibson

RISING ★ STARS

ISBN: 9781510444287

Text © 2019 Joe Craig
Illustrations, design and layout © 2019 Rising Stars UK Ltd
First published in 2019 by Rising Stars UK Ltd

Rising Stars UK Ltd, part of Hodder Education Group
An Hachette UK Company
Carmelite House, 50 Victoria Embankment, London, EC4Y 0DZ

www.risingstars-uk.com

Impression number 10 9 8 7 6 5 4 3 2 1
Year 2023 2022 2021 2020 2019

Author: Joe Craig
Series Editor: Sasha Morton
Publisher: Helen Parker
Illustrator: Dylan Gibson
Educational Consultant: Pauline Allen
Design concept: Julie Joubinaux
Page layout: Sarah Garbett @ Sg Creative Services
Editorial: Rachel Nickolds, Jennie Clifford and Michelle Daley

With thanks to the schools that took part in the development of *Reading Planet KS2*, including: Ancaster CE Primary School, Ancaster; Downsway Primary School, Reading; Ferry Lane Primary School, London; Foxborough Primary School, Slough; Griffin Park Primary School, Blackburn; St Barnabas CE First & Middle School, Pershore; Tranmoor Primary School, Doncaster; and Wilton CE Primary School, Wilton.

A catalogue record for this title is available from the British Library.

Printed in the United Kingdom

Orders: Please contact Bookpoint Ltd, 130 Park Drive, Milton Park, Abingdon, Oxon OX14 4SE. Telephone: (44) 01235 400555. Email: primary@bookpoint.co.uk.

CONTENTS

WORLD OF ROBOTS

Humans had to leave the planet fast. In the rush, a lot got left behind – including Jango and his grandpa. Now they're stuck on a world that's almost completely flooded.

Robotic ships roam the ocean. They gather up anything they find, put it into crates and bring it to the docks, where Jango, his grandpa and Izza have to sort it all out in their warehouse.

They find the good stuff that can be used in the space stations. They recycle the rest. Every few weeks, a transporter comes to take the good stuff up to the space stations.

But sometimes things go wrong …

Plan of the docks

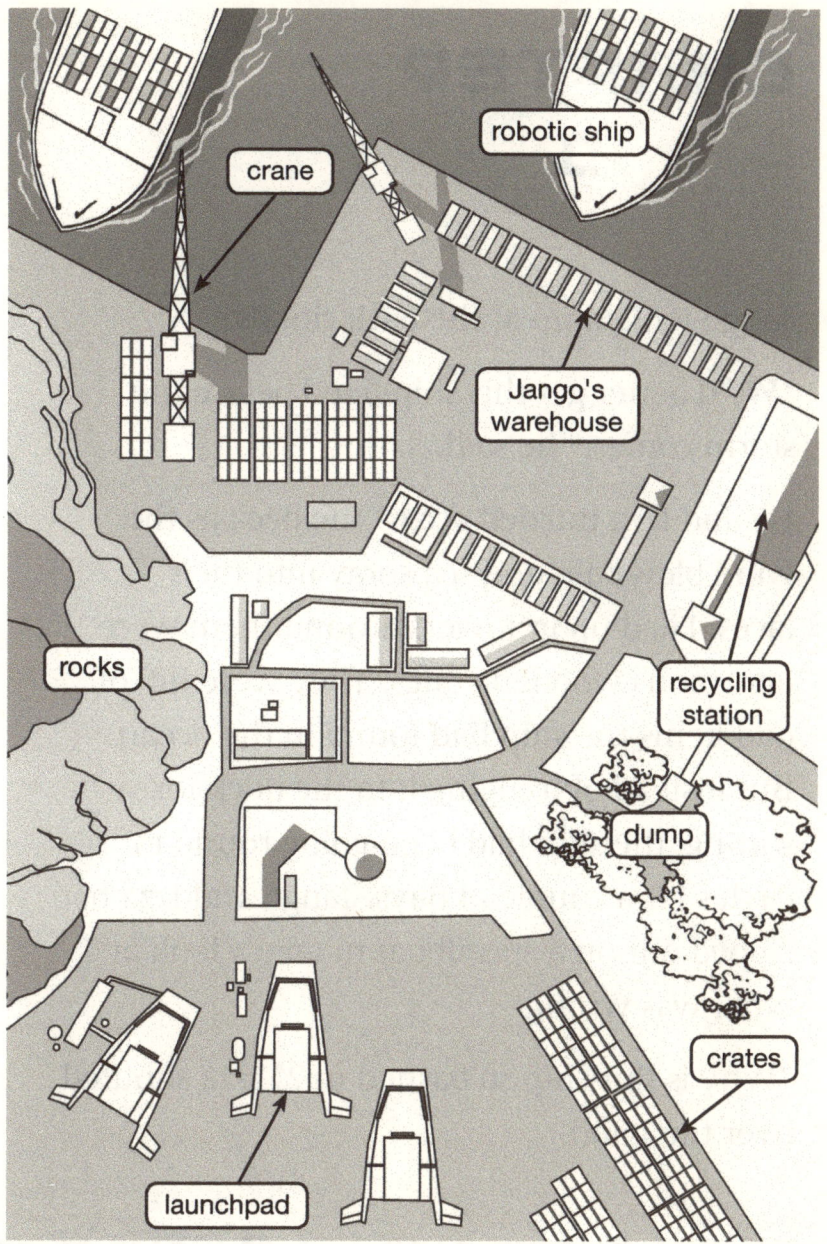

crane

robotic ship

Jango's warehouse

rocks

recycling station

dump

crates

launchpad

CHAPTER 1

Jango looked up at the dark clouds.

"We'd better get this ship fixed before the storm comes," he said.

He and Izza hurried across the deck as the wind blew rain and sea spray into their faces. Piled up in towers around them were enormous wooden crates. They were full of odd items the ship had found in the ocean. But instead of bringing it to the dock for sorting, the ship had been going round in circles for a couple of days. Jango and Izza had zipped out on a speedboat to take a look at what was wrong.

"Why is this ship so bashed up?" Izza shouted over the wind.

Jango yelled back, "There's nobody left to look after these ships out on the ocean. Just their old robot brains telling them what to do."

"I hope my robot brain doesn't end up like this," said Izza. She threw a clump of seaweed over the side. Then she grabbed the railing of the ship and rattled it. It was so rusty that a long piece of it snapped off in her hand.

They climbed up to a small room right at the top of the ship with windows on every side and a giant control desk. Jango pulled some tools from his fix-it bag. Izza was already tapping at the controls.

"This shouldn't take long," she said.

"Good," said Jango. He looked out at the clouds. They were even thicker and darker now, and rain hammered on the windows. "That storm is getting–"

Suddenly, a gigantic wave threw the ship to one side. Jango and his tools slid along the floor and clattered against the wall. Izza clung to the control desk.

"Woah," she said. "Do you think our speedboat is going to be …" Too late. Their little boat was already tumbling away in the waves. Beyond that, the dock was getting smaller and smaller.

"Don't worry," said Izza. "When I've fixed the ship's system, I'll tell it to take us home. I'll send a signal to your grandpa and he'll have snacks waiting for us. No problem."

"No problem," said Jango, nervously. He tried to get to his feet, but an even stronger wave made the ship lurch again. Jango slipped and landed with a bump.

"Are you just going to sit there?" asked Izza with a cheeky smile.

Before Jango could protest, there was a crash on the deck.

"What was that?" he asked.

"The storm is making a mess of all those crates," said Izza.

They both peered out of the window, through the hammering rain. On the deck, another pile of crates tumbled over. The top crate slid all the way across the deck. Izza and Jango couldn't see where it ended up, but they heard the crash of wood against metal. It rang out at the same moment as a deep roll of thunder.

Izza reached forward and wiped condensation from the window. Now they could clearly see the broken slats and snapped wood that used to be a crate. Then a wave came and washed it all overboard. A shadow seemed to leap out of the wreckage.

"What was that?" said Jango.

"It looks like something came from inside the crate," said Izza.

"It looked big."

"And fast."

"Do you think it's gone?"

"I don't know. I didn't–"

Something scratched at the door of the control room. Then there was a huge clap of thunder and the door burst open. There in the doorway, framed by the storm and a flash of lightning, stood an enormous, black and white tiger. The tops of its shoulders were at Jango's eye level. The width of its head alone was almost enough to fill the doorway.

Jango and Izza froze. The tiger's green eyes looked each of them up and down. Its nose twitched and its tongue flicked out, as if it was tasting their scent. They backed away slowly.

"Were you going to say it looked a bit like a really big tiger?" asked Izza quietly.

"I …" Jango whispered. "Yes, I was going to say that."

"I thought so. We should probably get out of here."

The tiger prowled closer.

"Any idea how?" said Jango.

CHAPTER 2

The colossal tiger blocked the doorway.

"Maybe we can distract it?" suggested Izza.

Jango couldn't take his eyes off the beast. He edged backwards. His heel nudged his fix-it bag. He reached down slowly and rummaged around inside it. The tiger took a deep breath and snorted. Puffs of steam came out of its nostrils as it crouched, ready to pounce.

Jango's hand found a rope. Almost without thinking, he threw it to the other side of the control room. The tiger's eyes shifted. It jumped for the rope like a kitten pouncing on a ball of wool.

"Go!" said Jango.

They scrambled out of the control room and down to the deck. Waves washed over them and water poured over their feet. In a sudden rush of movement, a crate slid straight at them. They dodged and watched it crash through the rusty railing, into the ocean.

Izza and Jango were soaked to the skin now. The storm was too loud for them to shout to each other, so Izza waved her arms to signal that they needed to get inside again. They sloshed along the deck. Izza hauled open a hatch and they hurtled down the stairs into a long, narrow corridor, closing the hatch behind them. Now they had some shelter, but the floor of the corridor was already flooded and water was still pouring through the edges of the hatch. They held on to the walls to stay steady while the ship rolled from side to side.

"Why was there a giant tiger inside that crate?" asked Jango.

"It can't be a real one," said Izza.

"It looked real to me," said Jango. "Especially around the teeth."

"I think it's a robot."

"A robot tiger?" Jango thought back to the way it had looked – the bright green eyes, the fine whiskers, the powerful muscles in its shoulders that made ripples in its fur when it moved. It all looked so real. But then, Izza looked like a real human and she was a robot.

"Who would make a robot tiger?" said Jango. "It's not going to fly a spaceship or be useful, like you."

"It's not supposed to be useful," said Izza. "When humans had to leave the planet, they couldn't take all the animals with them. Space is no place for tigers."

"So they made robot tigers to replace the real ones?" asked Jango.

"Exactly. They needed to show what life used to be like, including everything from the natural world. If the humans were able to take real animals, they did. Some were too big or too dangerous, and some were already extinct, so they made robot versions of those ones. Now, animals are kept in a kind of living museum. This one must have been left behind."

Like me, thought Jango. For a second, he felt a rush of sympathy for the tiger. It was out of place in the universe too. Then he remembered the hungry look in its eyes.

"So," he began, "if it's a robot, can it still eat us?"

"It'll probably try," said Izza. "It doesn't know it's a robot, does it? It thinks it's a real tiger."

"That's not good. By the time it finds out it can't eat us, we'll be … all chewed up."

"We need to get off this ship. But–" Before Izza could finish, there was a thud on the hatch. Then there was a softer noise amid the creaking sounds of the ship in the storm: a deep breath, then a snort. Jango thought he saw two puffs from the tiger's nostrils coming through the cracks of the hatch. It was right above them. It started scratching at the hatch, trying to get in.

"It knows we're here," said Izza.

"I think it has our scent," said Jango.

Izza looked each way down the corridor. The water level was nearly at their knees now. There was no other way out. But there was a way down.

"I've got a plan," she said. "If we stand on either side of the hatch, it won't be able to chase both of us."

"You're going to let it come down here?"

"We have to," said Izza. "At the rate this corridor is filling up, we'll drown before it moves."

"Good point. So what's the plan?"

"You stand one side, I'll stand the other side," said Izza. "We let the tiger down and it'll chase one of us. The other one can get back up on to the deck and look for some kind of controller for the tiger. Something that will send a signal to shut it down. It must have one. It would be a basic safety feature on any robot animal meant for space."

"OK," said Jango, taking a deep breath. The tiger scratched faster at the hatch, then started pounding it. Its paw was so strong that the hinges bent. "So, one of us gets up on to the deck," said Jango. "What does the other one do?"

"Gets away as fast as possible," said Izza. "Obviously."

"Out-run a robot tiger?"

"Not out-run … out-swim." Izza kicked one leg up to splash Jango. She had a huge grin on her face.

"How come you are enjoying this so much?" asked Jango.

Izza shrugged. "Maybe I don't understand fear the way humans do."

"Well, a bit of fear might be useful right now."

"Don't worry," said Izza. "If the tiger's chasing you, head down the stairs at the end of this corridor. I'll bet they lead to the engine room. It'll be flooded by now. Use the space there to swim around in a circle, then head back up here. Then you can climb out of the hatch and trap the tiger below deck. Ready?"

"I don't think I'll ever be. But here goes."

CHAPTER 3

Jango pushed the hatch open and jumped back at the same time. That moment, the tiger splashed down into the corridor. The splash mixed with the rain that was pouring in from above. When the water cleared, Jango saw that the giant beast was facing Izza.

"Go!" she yelled. She started splashing away down the corridor.

Jango jumped, landed one foot on the tiger's back to push off, out of the hatch. But the tiger's fur was slick. Jango slipped all the way up its back. His foot caught on something and he nearly tripped, but he grabbed the handrail of the rusty metal staircase and pulled himself up. When he looked back, the tiger was pounding down the corridor after Izza.

Jango caught his breath. The storm raged around him so it was hard to see anything. He picked his way through bits of soggy, broken wood, looking for some kind of controller to shut the tiger down. Every time the ship rolled, crates slid past him and bashed into each other. It felt like he was taking forever. It was useless. With so much of the crate washed overboard, what were the chances that the controller was still on the deck?

Suddenly, he heard Izza shouting. He turned and saw her racing towards him – with the tiger right behind her.

"Ruuuuun!" she yelled.

They splashed as fast as they could across the deck, ducking left and right, dodging

the sliding crates. The crates slowed the tiger down just enough for them to reach the ship's control room again. Jango slammed the door behind them. This time he locked it.

"What happened?" he said, panting. "I thought you were going to–"

"Trap it below deck?" said Izza. She was panting too, and even more soaked than Jango. "Hmm, our plan had a slight error."

"What?"

"It turns out tigers are really good swimmers."

Jango smacked his hand against his forehead. "So, you don't understand fear and you don't know anything about tigers," he groaned.

"I never said I was perfect," Izza shrugged. "What now?"

They looked down at the deck. The tiger seemed to be sheltering from the storm. It was lying between two crates, licking its paws.

"Wait," said Jango. "I think I've got it!" He grabbed the ship's binoculars and focused on the tiger. "When I jumped off the tiger's back, my foot caught on something."

"You jumped off its back?" said Izza. "What were you doing on its back?"

"Never mind that. I think it's wearing a collar!"

"A collar?"

"Yes, look!" Jango handed the binoculars to Izza. She looked closely. Jango was right.

Round the tiger's neck was a blue strap, almost hidden in its fur. And attached to the strap was …

"The controller!" Izza cried. "It must have got knocked when the crate broke open and switched him on. Do you think we can get it?"

"We'll need to get close enough to hit the right button and switch the tiger off again." Jango looked round the control room for something that would help. His fix-it bag was right where he'd left it. In the opposite corner was that length of rope.

"Right," he said. "New plan coming up."

CHAPTER 4

"Keep watching it," said Jango. "If it decides to come up here again, we've got to close this door quickly."

They had the door of the control room open just a crack. Jango was holding one end of the rusty railing Izza had broken off the ship. It went through the open door, and on the other end Jango had attached the rope. On the rope, he'd tied a hook from his fix-it bag to make a really big fishing rod, which was now dangling in the water.

"Are you sure tigers like fish?" asked Izza.

"I didn't know tigers could swim until a few minutes ago, so … no, I'm not sure," said Jango. "We just want to give it something to chew on. Then one of us can creep up,

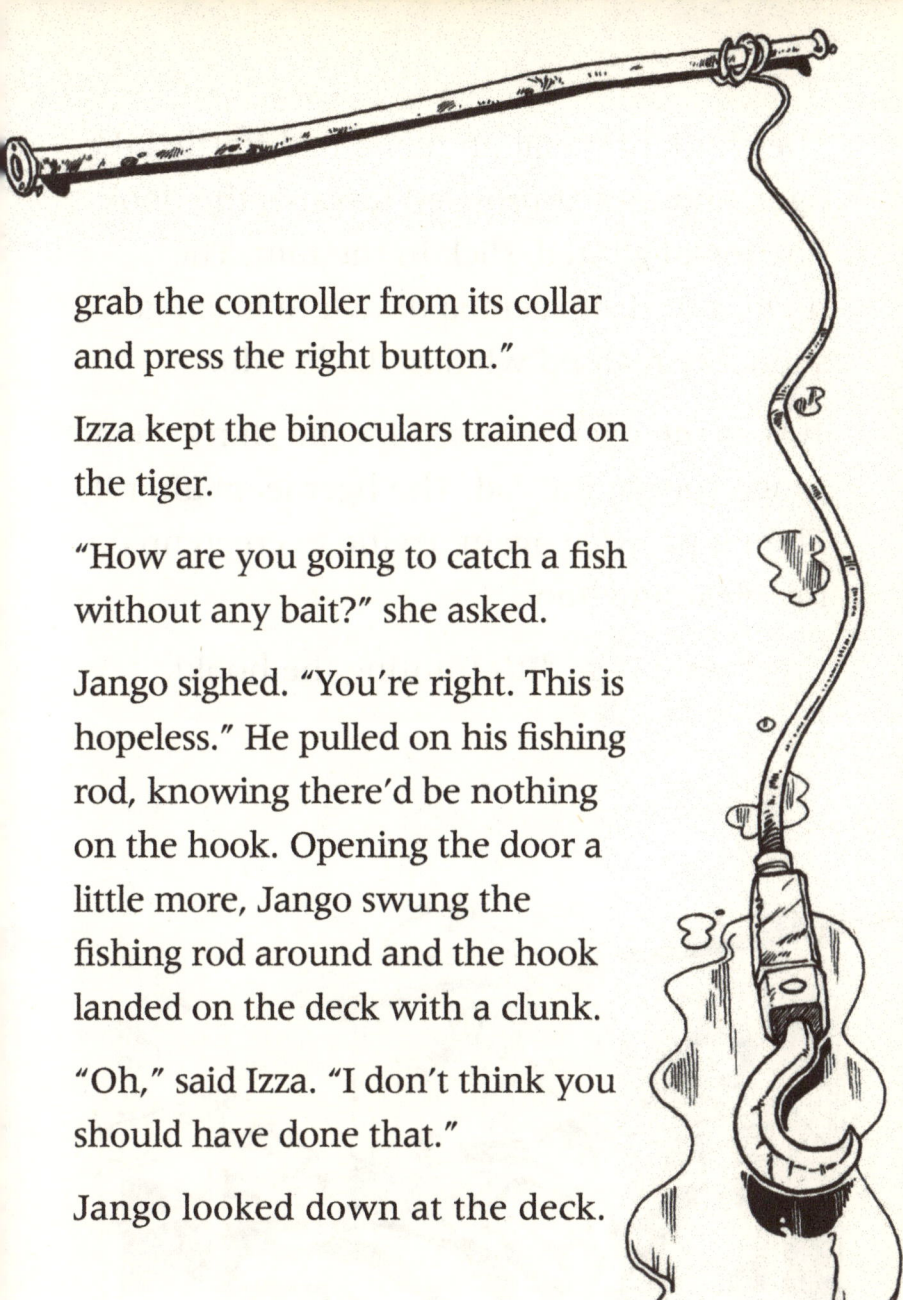

grab the controller from its collar and press the right button."

Izza kept the binoculars trained on the tiger.

"How are you going to catch a fish without any bait?" she asked.

Jango sighed. "You're right. This is hopeless." He pulled on his fishing rod, knowing there'd be nothing on the hook. Opening the door a little more, Jango swung the fishing rod around and the hook landed on the deck with a clunk.

"Oh," said Izza. "I don't think you should have done that."

Jango looked down at the deck.

The clunk of metal on metal had startled the tiger, and now it prowled towards the hook. The metal glinted, slick in the rain. The huge, wet tiger seemed drawn to it. Jango suddenly realised what he had to do.

Just as the tiger pounced for the shiny metal, Jango tugged the rod. The tiger leapt after it. Then it prowled again, trying to creep up on the gleaming hook.

"Yes!" said Izza. "It's hunting the hook! Bring it closer."

Bit by bit, Jango lured the tiger closer towards the control room. Each time it pounced for the hook, Jango tugged the rod. Eventually, the tiger was close enough that they could hear it purring. But it wasn't interested in eating them. It was completely fascinated by the shiny hook that Jango was making dance on the end of his fishing rod.

"Now, hold it high," said Izza. "Just out of reach, so it lifts its head …"

Jango leaned back to lift the other end of the rod higher. The tiger stood up on its back legs, with its front paws patting the air. Izza opened the door of the control room wider, without making a sound – without breathing. She reached for the tiger's collar. The tiger tottered on its back legs as Izza gripped the small square of plastic that was the tiger's controller. Slowly, she unclipped it.

A huge wave rocked the ship. The tiger staggered backwards. Jango lost his balance too, and let go of the fishing rod. It flew out of the door and knocked into Izza's hand. The tiger's controller jumped out of her fingertips. It seemed to hang in mid-air for a moment. Jango watched in despair as Izza tried to grab it again, but it slipped from her grasp. The controller fell to the deck, bounced, then dropped into the ocean.

Izza and Jango rolled on to their backs in the control room with a groan.

"We were so close!" wailed Izza. "Just that tiny controller was all we needed to send a signal!"

"We're never going to shut that tiger down!" said Jango. Then … "Wait! We don't need the controller to send a signal." He pointed at the ship's control desk. "We can send one from there. You said if you fixed it, you'd send a signal to Grandpa. You know, so he'd have snacks waiting for us when the ship took us home. If you can send a signal to the dock, you should be able to send a signal to the tiger to shut it down."

"Yes!" Izza leaped to the controls.

"Can you do it?"

"The signal won't be exact. I don't know what type of signal the tiger is set up to receive. But if I send out a wide signal that most robots would pick up ..."

"That'll work?" asked Jango.

"It should." Izza's hands were already flying across the controls.

"What if other things pick up the wide signal?" asked Jango.

"Everything in the area will pick it up," said Izza. "But that's okay. It's not like there are any other tigers around."

CHAPTER 5

"Done it," Izza announced at last. She stepped back from the ship's controls, and she and Jango both looked out at the deck. The tiger was lying down, licking its paws again.

"Why is it still awake?" asked Jango.

"I don't know," said Izza. "I'll try to boost the signal." She tapped at the controls again.

"I think it's getting something," said Jango. The tiger was standing up now. It started clawing at the crates around it.

Izza's face creased in concentration and her tongue stuck out to one side.
"Just one more thing ..."

Suddenly, the crate next to the tiger burst open. Through the storm, Jango saw a huge, dark figure rising up from the wooden box.

"Oh no," he said. "I think we just woke up a bear."

The bear stretched, and roared louder than the thunder. The tiger didn't like that. It reared up. Jango dreaded what was about to happen, but both animals stopped. They were distracted by the creaking and cracking of another crate … and another one … and another one …

All around them, crate after crate burst open. Out came all the robot animals that humans had built sanctuaries for up in space. Bears, lions, alligators, hippos, leopards, emus, zebras, moose, buffalo, jaguars ... there must have been a hundred of them, all running loose and panicking about being trapped on a tilting ship in the middle of a storm.

"Oops," said Izza.

"We have to get off this ship," said Jango.

"I can fix this. I know what I did wrong. I just need to–"

A rhino smashed through the window of the control room. Jango and Izza pounded back down to the deck and ran in different directions. The noise of the storm mixed with the cackles and roars of an entire jungle. Jango slid between a panda and a hyena who were sniffing at each other. Then an alligator reared up and snapped at him.

Just in time, Jango threw himself on to the back of the closest creature that wasn't going to try to eat him – a kangaroo. He clung to its fur and, together, they bounced over and between the other animals. When he was close enough, Jango pushed himself back and slid across the rain-lashed deck to reach Izza.

Izza had managed to reach the rope they'd used on their home-made fishing rod. Quickly, she tied it round Jango's waist, then round her own. She swung the hook round her head.

"What are we doing?" cried Jango. Izza's movements had the confidence of someone with a plan.

"We're going fishing." Izza threw the hook. Jango turned to see what she was trying to catch, and his eyes grew wide with astonishment. A huge black bear was pacing towards an enormous, slick, silver beast: a great white shark.

Izza's rope wrapped itself round the shark's fin. Before Jango could protest, Izza dragged the shark across the deck towards them. It struggled, and tried to get back towards the bear. To Jango's relief, that meant he and Izza were at the other end to all those teeth.

When it was close enough, Izza secured the rope round the shark's tail. Finally, Jango noticed what Izza had already worked out – around the shark's tail was a blue collar.

Just like every other animal in all those crates, the shark was wearing its own controller. Izza reached over and gripped the small, blue square. Now she had the right controller in her hand, it was easy to tell the shark what to do. She tapped the controls and yelled, "Hold on!"

The shark lurched forwards. It smashed through the ship's railing and into the water. Jango prepared himself to be dragged under the water. But Izza had control. She steered the shark expertly over the waves as if it was the speedboat they'd lost. Jango clung to the rope, snatching gasps of air between mouthfuls of seawater. Was Izza's plan actually going to work?

CHAPTER 6

They reached the dock, where Jango's grandpa was waiting for them. He was leaning on his mop.

"I'm sure I sent you out in a boat," he said. "That doesn't look like my boat." He waved his mop at the shark, which Izza had switched off with the controller. She and Jango left it floating beside the dock as they scrambled up the ladder and rushed to the warehouse with Grandpa scurrying after them.

"Sorry, Grandpa," said Jango, panting. "We had a bit of trouble on the ship."

"You mean … that ship?" Jango's grandpa turned and pointed his mop out to sea. The storm was blowing the ship towards the dock – along with all its wild animal passengers.

What would happen if the animals escaped on to dry land?

Izza ran up to the main signal desk in the warehouse and connected the shark's controller.

"I know what I did wrong before," she said, tapping the controls quicker than any human could.

"I don't want to hurry you," said Jango. "But the ship's about to get here. With all those animals on it."

A few minutes later, the ship bobbed into the dock. All was silent. Even the storm seemed to be backing away.

Izza and Jango stood on the edge of the dock, wet through to their bones. They looked out over the ship's deck. Hundreds of wild animals lay curled up, as if they were taking a nap together. All except one. The enormous, black and white tiger stretched out, yawned and hopped off the ship on to the dock to find somewhere warmer to sleep.

It took all night to get the robot animals into fresh crates. The beasts were so heavy, Izza and Jango could only shift them with help from Unit – their self-driving robot truck. A week later, a transporter came down and took on enough animals to fill a small jungle. They were all heading for new homes on the space station, where humans could marvel at the creatures that had lived in the old days. These were important memories for the human race. Izza and Jango watched the transporter disappear into the clouds.

After a minute, they walked back to Unit, who was waiting to take them to the warehouse. Curled up in the warmest spot under Unit's engine was the tiger.

"You're sure you can reprogram it to be totally safe?" Jango asked.

"You don't reprogram pets," said Izza. "You train them."

Jango smiled and nodded.

"You're right," he said. "Space is no place for tigers."

Now answer the questions ...

1 The author uses words like 'thicker and darker' to describe the clouds out at sea in Chapter 1. What does this suggest about the weather at the start of the story?

2 What reason does Izza give for not being afraid of the tiger chasing her in Chapter 2?

3 Which part of the story best describes what was inside the crates?

4 Find a word in Chapter 5 that means 'places where animals are cared for'.

5 Why was it important that Jango jumped off the tiger's back during the story?

6 What did you think Jango's new plan was going to be at the end of Chapter 3?

7 Was Grandpa concerned about Jango and Izza returning to the dock on a robot shark? How can you tell?

8 Which scene from the story did you think was the most dramatic, and why?